EMPIRES OF INDIA
THE RAJPUTS
ADAPTED FROM ORIGINAL
AMAR CHITRA KATHA COMICS

EMPIRES OF INDIA
THE RAJPUTS

ADAPTED FROM ORIGINAL
AMAR CHITRA KATHA COMICS

Written by: **Shikha Lal**

Published by
Rupa Publication India Pvt. Ltd.
7/ 16, Ansari Road, Daryaganj, New Delhi 110002

First published by Rupa Publication India Pvt. Ltd.
In collaboration with Amar Chitra Katha Pvt. Ltd. 2024

Sales centres:
Bengaluru, Chennai
Hyderabad, Jaipur, Kathmandu
Kolkata, Mumbai, Prayagraj

Text and illustrations copyrights © Amar Chitra Katha Private Limited 2024
AMAR CHITRA KATHA PVT LTD
Office no. 5017/18/19/20, 1AEROCITY NIBR Corporate Park,
Andheri-Kurla Road, Safed Pool Shivaji Nagar,
Jarimari Sakinaka, Mumbai 400072

Designed by Manoj Tandel
Art Director – Ketan Tondwalkar

Adapted from the original ACK Comics
Original Illustrations
Rana Kumbha – H. S. Chavan
Rana Sanga – Ram Waeerkar
Rana Pratap & Chattrasal – Pratap Mulick

All rights reserved.
No part of this publication may be reproduced, transmitted,
or stored in a retrieval system, in any form or by any means,
electronic, mechanical, photocopying, recording or otherwise,
without the prior permission of the publisher.

P-ISBN: 978-93-6156-941-8
E-ISBN: 978-93-6156-128-3

First impression 2024

10 9 8 7 6 5 4 3 2 1

Moral rights of the author has been asserted.

Printed in India
This book is sold subjected to the condition that it shall not, by
way of trade or otherwise, be lent, resold, hired out, or otherwise
circulated, without the publisher's prior consent, in any form of
binding or cover other than that in which it is published.

CONTENTS

1	Victory Forever	7
2	The Heir Returns	41
3	The Battle of Haldighati	73
4	The Making of Rana Chattrasal	94

VICTORY FOREVER

Rana Kumbha was immersed in playing his veena. His hands moved expertly over the strings, beautiful melodies filling up the chamber. It was, therefore, with great reluctance, that a messenger interrupted the Mewar ruler's relaxation time.

"Your majesty," he said with a bow.

Rana Kumbha stopped playing and set aside his veena carefully. He walked over to another seat and leaned back in it comfortably before motioning for the messenger to continue.

The messenger cleared his throat and said, "Mahpa has recently been spotted."

The Chittor ruler asked, "Where?"

"In Mandu, according to our sources."

Rana Kumbha's eyes lit up with the fire of revenge. That name had always been in his thoughts since he was 15 years old. "Your time has come, Mahpa," he silently vowed.

Everyone in the kingdom knew that this man was wanted. Rana Kumbha was not one to

forget or forgive betrayals, especially not someone who had killed his own father. As a young boy, he had learnt much from his father, Maharana Mokal, and looked up to him. His heart broke when his father had ordered that he escape when Mahpa had assaulted them along with Chacha and Mera.

The other two had been found and killed after Kumbha had ascended the throne, but Mahpa had managed to evade them and gone into hiding. The ruler had promised himself that he would avenge his father's death.

"It seems his time is finally up," Rana Kumbha remarked. "I will ask Sultan Mahmud Khilji to return the criminal to us."

Promptly, an envoy was sent to Mandu with the request.

Days passed and the envoy finally returned. Rana Kumbha was sitting with his uncle, Rao

Ran Mal, when the man walked in to deliver the sultan's reply.

"Your majesty, the sultan has said that Mahpa is now under his protection and he will not send him back here," the envoy stated.

"He'd rather protect a murderer?" Rana Kumbha frowned. He was irritated but he wasn't going to let anybody deny him his rightful vengeance.

He stood up and turned to his uncle. "Well, if the Sultan won't send Mahpa to Chittor, then we'll just have to go get him from Mandu, won't we?"

In agreement, Rao Ran Mal and the forces of Rana Kumbha eventually marched towards Mandu, determined to fulfil their mission.

Sultan Khilji dispatched his own army to tackle the Rajputs. He relished the idea of crushing them.

"Oh, looks like the little Rajput's ego has been hurt," Khilji chuckled. "His childishness shall be the end of him. And that will open up Mewar to us — all gains, as far as I can see."

His commanders were of the same opinion and marched confidently to counter the Rajput forces.

They met Rana Kumbha's army at Sarangpur, a place that lay between Chittor and Mandsaur. The battle that ensued was fierce. Swords clashed and the sultan's army found that the Rajputs' cavalry was equally skilled as theirs. Bit by bit, Khilji's army had to retreat. Their weapons and skills proved no match for Rana Kumbha's men. Aware that they now had a clear advantage, the Rajputs pressed on. It was time to make the enemy yield.

Sultan Khilji found himself and his men surrounded. Rana Kumbha had laid siege to the fort of Mandu where they now sat.

"The nerve!" Khilji fumed. He was very upset with the Mewar ruler, but even more so with his own forces for failing to prevent the current situation. It was an embarrassment, and over what — one disposable man! But he did know one thing, that Rana Kumbha

was nothing if not patient; he had waited for years to find Mahpa. This meant that he would have no problem letting the current siege go on. The sultan decided to sleep over it. "Sometimes the best course of action comes to you when you're in a slightly more relaxed state," he decided.

Unfortunately for him, he misjudged Rana Kumbha's line of thought. The very next day,

Rajput forces stormed the fort. Khilji found himself a prisoner of Rana Kumbha.

Rana Kumbha calmly looked at him and said, "You know that all this was avoidable. Anyway, I now give you the opportunity to do what you refused to do back then — hand Mahpa over."

At first Khilji was surprised. Then his face broke into a wry smile and he chuckled. "It seems I still get to have the last laugh. You have me, but not Mahpa!"

"You helped him escape?"

The sultan shook his head. "I simply told him that I could no longer shield him. He was free to plan his escape however he could," Khilji gleefully relayed, determined to dampen any sense of victory that the Rajput had.

The Mewar king only shrugged and said, "We will find him — if he's still alive, that is."

The pieces of Mahpa's escape came together after an investigation. The real turnaround was when they found a dead horse near one of the fort's walls. Judging by the height of the wall, it was clear that the horse was killed on impact. On being interrogated, Khilji's men confirmed that Mahpa had ridden away on this very horse. He had obviously attempted to jump down while riding his horse. Unsteady footprints in the ground hinted that Mahpa had somehow survived the fall. He still remained elusive. So, Rana Kumbha would have to wait to avenge his father. He was not a king to dwell on what was momentarily out of his hands. Trusting that his spies would do the needful to locate Mahpa, he returned to Chittor with another plan in mind.

"I am incredibly proud of you all," he announced to his army and the general public. "To commemorate this amazing victory of ours, I have decided to have a tower built here at Chittorgarh: Vijay Stambh!"

The title was apt – vijay meant 'victory' and stambh meant 'pillar'. Sutradhar Jaita was the architect who was entrusted with this responsibility. He and his three sons set out to design and build a piece that would be remembered for generations to come. Talented, skilled artisans and sculptors from near and far came to work on the tower. For them, it was more than a project.

"Sultan Khilji has taken over so much of central, south, and eastern India," one of the sculptors chatted with a fellow worker. "Only one person has singlehandedly stopped him in his tracks when it's come to the west – Rana Kumbha!" His eyes gleamed with pride.

"Absolutely," his companion nodded in agreement. "Imagine what our lives would have been if this madman had been able to expand to the west as well. It would be nothing short of hell. I've heard the whispers from other provinces. Imagine if our king wasn't a brave and daring man!"

"The best part though — now he's got Khilji at his mercy!"

The Mewar ruler was a hero in the eyes of the public. Sutradhar Jaita wanted to do justice to just how great a leader he was. He wanted the tower to not only be symbolic of the victory in the battle of Sarangpur but also be a homage to the king, his vision, his ideals, and his talents. It was going to be slow work but he was going to ensure this would be a masterpiece, come what may.

Six months passed... Khilji heard footsteps approaching and straightened up. Two armed guards approached him and asked

him to come with them. They led him straight to Rana Kumbha then.

"Wonder what he wants now..." thought Khilji.

"You must be wondering why I have summoned you," the king read his mind.

When his prisoner said nothing, Rana Kumbha continued, "Today is your lucky day. I have decided to set you free."

Khilji was taken by surprise, but kept a straight face. There was more.

"I have also decided to return Mandu to you. I have only one condition — that you never shelter a murderer again."

Khilji bowed, "You are gracious, Rana. I had heard a lot about you and your sense of fairness, but now I have experienced it myself. I give you my word. It will be as you have asked."

Khilji was glad at the opportunity that had presented itself. "Fool! Not that I'm complaining..." he thought. "Let me just regain charge, Rana. I will avenge this humiliation. Then you can curse yourself for the rest of your life for committing this blunder when everything was actually in your favour."

Though others were unhappy with his decision to free Khilji, Rana Kumbha was firm that it was in line with dharma. The king then busied himself with dealing with the rebellions in his kingdom. While he had been engaged in the siege of Mandu, some of his vassals had decided to rebel and claim independence. Even without his uncle, who had passed away by this time, the Rajput king was able to quash these rebellions with ease.

He was in Haravati, punishing one such errant vassal in 1444, when news from Chittor reached him.

"Ranaji, Sultan Khilji's army is ransacking the outskirts of Mewar," the messenger said. He reported cases of plundered temples, much to the anger of the Rajput ruler. He decided that Khilji needed another lesson in humility.

And so it was that he battled the Sultan again near a place called Mandalgarh. The Rajputs proved to be a force to reckon with and Khilji had to retreat quickly back to his kingdom, biding his time until he found another opportunity to somehow get even.

But time was not on his side. Instead, Rana Kumbha was presented with a unique chance while he was at Kumbhalgarh, a beautiful fort built on the western range of the Aravali Hills.

"Your majesty, the Sultan of Nagaur seeks an audience with you," said a guard, coming into his chambers.

Curious, the king allowed Shamskhan in. "I seek your refuge and help, Ranaji," the Sultan wasted no time in getting to the point. "My brother, Mujahid Khan, has overthrown me and even attempted to take my life. If you help me regain my throne, I think we can establish friendly relations in the future."

It was an interesting proposition. The Sultanate of Nagaur to the north of Mewar had made several attempts earlier to attack and annex the region. Threats from the Delhi Sultanate in the north and those of Gujarat and Malwa from the south

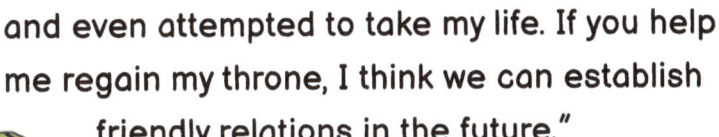

remained, but this was a chance to neutralise at least one of his enemies.

"I will help on one condition," Rana Kumbha declared. "You must acknowledge my supremacy by demolishing a part of the battlements of the Nagaur fort." Shamskhan agreed.

So it was that the Rajput army attacked Nagaur, forcing Mujahid Khan to flee. As promised, Shamskhan was given back his throne. However, he dillydallied on fulfilling his part of the deal. Instead, word got back to the Rana that Shamskhan had started to further fortify the defences.

"These sultans say anything to get what they want," Rana Kumbha observed. "Let's show them that we take our promises seriously." Soldiers understood what that comment meant.

Nagaur was attacked again, the fort destroyed and taken under Rana Kumbha's rule.

Shamskhan fled and sought help from the Sultan of Gujarat. While they did jointly try to reclaim the kingdom by luring the Rajput king away to a battle at another fort, they were outsmarted and defeated. Disappointed and battered, they retreated to Gujarat, leaving Nagaur firmly in Rajput possession.

The sculptor was putting finishing touches on the statue he had delicately carved out.

"Breathtaking!" a voice startled him. He looked up to see Rana Kumbha standing over his shoulder and admiring his work. Hurriedly, he got up to pay his respects.

As the man bowed, the king gently waved his hand to acknowledge him. "Please don't let me disturb you. Such art can only flow from divine energy. My wish was to dedicate this great structure to Lord Vishnu. You are turning that wish into a reality."

He looked with wonder and satisfaction at how the Vijay Stambh was taking shape. While five stories had already been completed, more individual stones with carvings

of Hindu gods and goddesses, legends and stories from the Ramayana and Mahabharata, weapons, and musical instruments were laid out on the ground. They were waiting to be assembled on subsequent floors.

Even unfinished, the structure looked exquisite. Set in red stone and white marble, it sported a balcony on every floor. There

were carvings both outside and inside the tower, with circular and narrow stairs within.

"There are more pieces, your majesty," the architect pointed in another direction. "Those are with stories of the conquests made by you and your ancestors, bringing glory to our land."

"I hope you have dedicated space to put in all these artists' stories too," the king said.

The architect nodded. "Just as you wanted."

In fact, the design also fully captured the Rajput king's love of literature, art, and music.

While the beautiful Vijay Stambh continued to be built day by day, something ugly was rearing its head elsewhere.

"Sultan Khilji has sent me with a proposal that he thinks would be in our collective

interest," said Tej Khan, the sultan's prime minister. "We believe that if the forces of Mandu and Gujarat join hands, we can easily defeat Kumbha."

The Sultan of Gujarat was silent, considering the idea. When he hadn't spoken in a while, Khilji's prime minister explained that the plan would be to capture Mewar and then split it equally between the sultanates.

"My enemy's enemy is my friend. I accept." The Gujarat Sultanate was eager to eliminate Rana Kumbha once and for all.

As the allied army advanced towards Mewar, spies relayed the message to the Rajput king. He wasted no time in mobilising his forces. This time, though, strategy was going to be more important than ever. The Gujarat Sultanate's army advanced towards Kumbhalgarh, while Khilji's men aimed straight for Chittor. Rana Kumbha knew he could not fight both simultaneously without losing significant men or ground. It would prove to be an impossible battle. Initially, he planned to send Khilji packing, but chose to tackle the army from Gujarat instead as he learnt that they were already near Kumbhalgarh. He clashed with them at Mandalgarh.

For a while, it seemed like the two armies were evenly matched. Both suffered losses, but towards the end of the second day, the numbers looked grim for the Rajputs.

"We have lost so many men and equipment," Rana Kumbha took stock of the situation.

"This is the right time to retreat, else the tide will turn against us irreversibly."

"Fall back!" he cried out to his men.

As night fell, they retreated into a hilly cavern in the Aravallis. This would prove to be an excellent decision as it strategically offered an advantage. The Rajputs knew these hills like the back of their hands and could launch a surprise attack. Morale was running low

among the ranks though, something the king sensed.

"My brave men," he spoke later that night to every soldier present. "I admit we have not had great success in beating back the enemy this time as we have in the past. But I do want you to remember that we have defeated this army before. We have done so because there is a fire in our hearts — to protect everything and everyone we hold dear! That fire, my men, is our strength. These animals will stop at nothing to destroy everything that we have built, nurtured, and protected with our lives. If we fail, we fail our

people, our families, and our way of life. We forfeit our freedom. Do we want that?"

"No!" came a resounding roar from the men.

"Will we let that happen?"

"No!"

"That's right. This cannot happen – not on our watch. If we lose this battle, the Sultan of Mandu will occupy Chittor. That is our sacred place – our land. Will we let them take it?"

"Never!"

"Then tomorrow morning we shall resume our attack with renewed strength. Let them think that we have lost heart. We will catch them unaware, and they will regret that they ever even thought of crossing the brave men of Mewar!"

"Jai Mewar!"

"Jai Ekalingji!"

True to their word, the Rajput army sprung a vicious attack on the Gujarat forces the next morning. The latter was terribly exposed, having decided to camp in the plains. It was too late before they realised that the enemy was so close. The Gujarat army was decimated.

Troubles for Mewar were far from over though. During this time, Khilji's men had already reached the Chittor fort and laid siege to it. Mandu's sultan wanted to conclude matters quickly. If his calculations were correct, he had a decent window to capture the fort, but he didn't want to take any chances. Having lost to Rana Kumbha multiple times already, he had learned not to underestimate him.

"You are a great warrior, Kumbha, I'll give you that," he spoke to himself as he stared at the fort that he was about to claim as his own.

"But I have done it right this time. All your best men must be with you to fend off the Gujarat Sultanate, so I doubt your few men here can hold out much longer. Either way, by the time you arrive – if you do at all – Chittor will be mine."

He ordered his army to march ahead. It was now time to set the final part of the plan into motion.

"What's that?" he heard a guard shout, pointing at a distance to the east.

A plume of dust appeared over the horizon and seemed to grow thicker by the second.

When the flag came into sight, Khilji gasped, "No, it can't be!"

Rana Kumbha and his men charged in, slicing through the Mandu forces with absolute rage. What was supposed to be an easy win for

Khilji turned out to be yet another humiliation as his army was brutally defeated. Left with no other choice, they hurried back to the safety of their own territory.

This battle went down in history and was celebrated throughout Mewar. It left Khilji so demoralised that he didn't even attempt attacking the region for the next ten years. Rana Kumbha grew even more in stature. Tales of his victories were etched into the Vijay Stambh. Completed in 1448, it rose 37 metres into the air and had nine stories in total. True to the architect's vision, it captured Rana Kumbha's reign and his spectacular achievements not just in war but also in literature, art, and music. As promised to the king, the architect and his sons' names were carved on the fifth floor while the name of Allah was carved in Arabic on the third and eighth floors. The topmost floor was dedicated to the Mewar king's family and their contributions. A total of 157 steps led up to the terrace from where one could see the entire city in all directions – great, sprawling and thriving. One look at the awe-inspiring Vijay Stambh would narrate the complete story of this great ruler, who – till his death – remained undefeated in all the wars he ever fought.

THE HEIR RETURNS

Holding the ladle, Sangram felt unsure for the first time in his life. It felt odd in his hand. He gave the pot a final stir, hoping that would do it. Though cooking was not exactly his strength, he was trying his best.

"Thoo!" his new acquaintance spat it out.

The other two managed to gulp a morsel down, but their expressions made it clear how they felt about it.

"It... needs something more," Ajay tried to give his feedback politely.

Mohan just nodded in agreement, but Rajat had no patience for diplomacy. "It needs salt, but more than that, it needs to be edible!"

Sangram apologised and promised to do better. The group decided to let it go. Perhaps he would be better at other tasks.

The next task was shepherding. Armed with a staff, Sangram attempted to keep the sheep and goats together as far as possible. Unfortunately, it seemed as though the animals knew that he had no prior experience in this. The sheep ignored him, and the goat even butted him a few times.

While it amused his fellow shepherds initially, they were soon annoyed when every day they had to run after the animals that had slipped past Sangram.

"He was supposed to help," Mohan muttered, exasperated.

Ajay conceded that the new entrant was less than an ideal addition. "I just thought perhaps he's got no one and is a bit challenged

without an eye. I genuinely felt he'd be good at something. How was I to know?"

"Very noble thought! I guess we all thought we'd give him a chance to prove himself, but let's face it, he's a bungling idiot," Rajat hissed. "I don't mind calling a spade a spade. He may be disabled but come on, he hasn't caught on to anything. At this rate, we've just got one more mouth to feed and we're doing all the work but getting little rest."

Ajay seemed to be a little undecided about Sangram but Rajat was adamant that the newcomer was a liability. "Oye," he called out to him.

Sangram sensed trouble as soon as he heard the tone. "Yes?" He approached the group, setting his staff aside on the ground.

Rajat said, "When we asked you if you could cook and graze our sheep and goats for us, clearly you lied."

"Actually, my exact words were 'I will try'," Sangram defended himself.

"Well, your attempt is pathetic," Mohan joined in. "It's been a week and I'm straining to see any improvement."

Sangram realised he was in danger of being kicked out from the group. He had no one else to turn to. His best bet was to apologise and try harder. Ajay had been silent all this while, but the disappointment was clear in his eyes. Sangram felt that perhaps he could still sway Ajay in his favour, so he tried his best in appealing to him for understanding his circumstances. Luckily, it worked!

Months passed and now even Ajay was convinced that they had made a mistake. "He

is absolutely good for nothing," he lamented. Now he didn't even bother to keep his voice down. Sangram could hear every word exchanged between the men.

"I always told you there was no point in keeping him," Rajat complained. Just seeing Sangram irritated him.

"With all those wounds he's got, I bet he's a runaway bandit," Mohan claimed. "Probably wasn't good at that either."

Sangram grew tired of listening to the snide remarks day in and day out. He was sure that this was now an unsustainable arrangement. They were unhappy with him and, admittedly, he was unhappy with them.

"I have to get another job," he thought.

It wasn't like he hadn't tried. Unfortunately, nothing had worked out so far. But if there was anything Sangram knew, it was that he was a survivor. He just had to persevere and something would come his way for sure. He inhaled deeply, as if in hope for better times.

A few days later, Sangram had wandered off to a slightly cut-off area where the animals were grazing when he heard a familiar sound – horse's hooves! He turned around to see two horses galloping towards him. Their riders had long spears in their hands.

"Armed horsemen!" Sangram noted, narrowing his eyes. "Maybe they are rebel Rajputs."

"Who are you?" one of the horsemen demanded as the other one started circling the shepherd.

Unsure of their identity, Sangram decided to play it safe. Resting his staff casually on

his shoulders, he answered, "I am Sangram Singh. I am also a Rajput, but I have no weapons even to protect myself."

It was an appeal to the Rajput code of honour. The horsemen paused, briefly observing the man before them. He was tall and definitely strongly built. The bandage across his eye showed he had had some tough experience in life, whether by accident or in war was yet to be ascertained. He had just mentioned that he didn't have a weapon, so there was a decent chance he actually knew how to use one. The horsemen had a silent exchange between them before one of them spoke, "We will give you arms. Why don't you join us?"

Sangram's heart leapt with joy. "With pleasure!" he smiled. His luck seemed to have finally turned.

Piercing eyes measured him up and down. Sangram felt very exposed suddenly, and that was saying something, given that he was otherwise a fearless man. The bearded man was the Rajputs' leader, that much was clear. His bright eyes were intelligent and playful at the same time, yet you somehow knew that if you did something wrong, they'd harden into an unforgiving glare in an instant.

"I am Karam Chand," he introduced himself. "My men tell me you are a brave Rajput and want to join us."

"Yes, I do," Sangram answered. He was not too keen to run after sheep and goats again. He was no shepherd!

"Let's hope you make a good dacoit then," Karam Chand said matter-of-factly, waving him away.

Sangram held his breath. "Dacoits! They are rebels who have turned dacoits…"

It wasn't quite what he had hoped for but he reminded himself that he didn't have an alternative. This opportunity had come after an agonising wait and several failures. On the bright side, he did possess the skills for the job.

A young lady entered the room at that moment. Karam Chand introduced her as his daughter and told Sangram that she would show him around and assist with any requirements. The daughter nodded politely, acknowledging the new member of their gang. She didn't speak much in her father's presence; instead, she simply gestured to Sangram to follow her.

Sangram felt guarded in the first few days as he adjusted to his new surroundings. Karam Chand doubted Sangram's ability to fight solely based on his word.

"So, do you think you can win a little match with one of our best?" the leader asked.

"Yes," Sangram kept his answer brief and firm.

"How about that eye?" Karam Chand smirked as he pointed to the bandaged eye.

"What about it?"

"Can you fight with it?"

"What makes you think I can't?"

Everyone standing around chuckled appreciatively at the young man's confidence.

Sangram was handed a sword. He accepted it almost reverentially. At last, his fingers curled around an object he knew and innately understood. He adjusted his grip on it and turned around to calmly size up his opponent. The bout began.

"You were spectacular," Karam Chand's daughter complimented Sangram after he had won not just one, but three bouts against different opponents.

The young man smiled, "Thank you. I hope I have proved myself to your father."

"Definitely," she answered. "Just as I was leaving, I heard him commenting to someone else that your one eye is..."

She paused, realising it could be rude to speak so casually about someone's disability.

Sangram raised his eyebrows quizzically only to have the lady look uncomfortable and embarrassed. He couldn't help himself and broke into a laugh, "It's okay, I promise I won't be offended."

She completed her sentence, "He said that your one eye is as good as two."

"Well, I'm glad he thinks so, although from personal experience I can tell you that I do miss the other one sometimes."

Karam Chand's daughter paused for a bit before saying, "If I may ask, what happened to your eye?"

"It's a long story. I will tell you some other time." Saying so, he took his leave.

Karam Chand was pleased with the latest addition to his group. Sangram displayed an excellent command over not just weapons but a deep understanding of strategy and motivating the men. With every successful hit, he'd grown to earn the respect of everyone around him. He was disciplined, would never leave a man behind, and always ensured that the job got done. What he didn't realise was that Sangram personally was not too happy. While he was glad that he had a roof over his head and regular food, he could not make peace with the fact that they were stealing. He was not proud of it at all. For him, the only bright spot was his growing friendship with the chief's daughter.

"What are you doing here alone?" She caught him sitting on a rock, gazing up into the sky one day.

"Thinking," he replied.

"What about?"

Sangram's shoulders drooped. "I do not like the life I am leading right now."

"Neither do I," she admitted. "Where is the Rajput honour in dacoity?"

Sangram stood up. "Then why don't you come with me? Let us get married and get away from all this."

While they were discussing their plans, one of the other rebels named Maru overheard their conversation.

He instantly reported it to Karam Chand. Livid, the chief asked Maru to keep an eye on Sangram.

A few days later, Maru urgently sought the chief's attention. Curious, Karam Chand followed him deep into the forest. There he found Sangram lying on the ground, sound asleep. Towering above his head was a snake.

Astounded, the two men froze.

"You know what this means, sir," Maru whispered. "It's a sign — Sangram is going to become a king."

Karam Chand was lost in thought. "My daughter could not have chosen a better partner for herself."

He swore Maru to secrecy. He couldn't tell anyone, even Sangram himself, about what they had witnessed in the jungle.

The following day, the chief confronted Sangram about how he didn't appreciate their way of life.

"It's not just me. Your daughter doesn't like it either," the young man boldly stated.

"So, you've been meeting each other, is it?" Karam Chand gruffly demanded.

"Yes, we wish to get married."

Karam Chand looked at Sangram. "Very well, you have my consent. Promise me that you will always keep her happy."

Delighted, Sangram vowed that he would do everything in his power to make sure that his wife remained content with her life.

The entire gang celebrated their marriage. After all the ceremonies were completed, the bride and groom approached Karam Chand for his blessings. Emotional, he placed a loving hand on both their heads, blessing them with a long, happy, and fulfilling married life. "One more thing, from now on, I appoint you, Sangram, as the naik of my band."

The bride and groom were surprised and exchanged looks. They thought it had been clear that they did not wish to continue living the dacoit life anymore.

"I'm sorry but I cannot accept that," Sangram finally spoke up.

"Why not? How do you intend to keep my daughter happy without holding a job?"

"I'm destined to rule over Mewar."

Gasps rippled through the crowd. Eyes widened. Even the bride looked at her husband in complete surprise.

Karam Chand understood the implication but wanted to be absolutely sure. He asked, "Rule over Mewar? Isn't that a vain hope?"

"No," Sangram stated simply. "Not for Rana Sanga, the eldest son of Rana Raimal."

Nobody could believe their ears. They had never known his true identity! All this while, the people of Mewar had believed that Rana Sanga was no more. How had he managed to escape death?

Rana Sanga now recounted his tale. As the eldest son of the ruling king, he was considered the true heir to the throne. However, his brothers Prithviraj and Jaimal constantly opposed his claim to the throne. It seemed that the smallest of things could trigger an argument among the brothers. Each argued that the other two were unfit to be rulers. One such day, the brothers were bitterly bickering when their uncle, Surajmal, suggested a way to resolve the issue.

"Let the oracle, Charani Devi, guide us," he said. "Her predictions are never wrong."

The trio agreed and on horseback rode to Charani Devi's temple. The priest there asked them to wait while he went to fetch the attendant who was the mouthpiece for the Devi's wishes.

"Sanga, if the prediction is not in your favour, what will you do?" Jaimal asked.

Sanga wasn't sure if it was the atmosphere of the temple or something else, but the answer came to him very easily: "If Mewar is not mine, then I will go away and establish a new kingdom of my own elsewhere."

"And if it is yours, then you'll have to kill me first," Prithviraj declared.

Sanga rolled his eyes and decided to just wait until the priest and attendant arrived. When asked the question again, she pointed to the tiger skin beneath Sanga.

"So that means I'll rule the kingdom," Sanga concluded.

"... of which I'll enjoy a share," Surajmal chimed in, pointing to his one knee partially resting on the same tiger skin.

Prithviraj was incensed, "So that's the game of the jackal!"

What happened next was a blur. Prithviraj attacked both Sanga and his uncle. Sanga managed to escape on his horse but Prithviraj drew his bow and arrow. He took his stance, took aim and let go. The arrow flew and hit the true heir squarely in the eye.

In agonising pain, Sanga was on the lookout for any kind of shelter. Both his brothers were pursuing him; he was losing blood profusely. Sanga knew it was only a matter of time

before he lost consciousness due to the severe blood loss. He was now in the border areas of Mewar.

As he grew faint, his horse slowed down and came to a halt in front of Veeda's house. A tradesman by profession, Veeda immediately recognised the prince. "My prince, you're badly wounded!" he exclaimed. He rushed to the prince's aid and instructed his wife to lead him to the stable behind their home. There, he urged Sanga to switch horses in a bid to throw the brothers off his tail.

"I escaped eventually but I heard later that Jaimal did not spare Veeda," Prince Sanga now neared the conclusion of his story. "I decided to go by the name Sangram Singh and be a shepherd. I knew that as long as Prithviraj remained determined to sit on the throne, this war over succession would help only Mewar's enemies. I simply could not let that happen," he said.

"So now your plan is to return to Chittor?" Karam Chand asked.

"Not yet," the prince answered. He wanted his identity to remain a secret for as long as possible. That was the only way he could ensure his protection until the time was right to go back.

Karam Chand immediately offered his resources. Touched, the prince accepted.

Years later, a messenger returned with interesting news: "The king's men are looking for you everywhere. Princes Prithviraj and Jaimal are no more. The time to go back and take the throne is here!"

Rana Sanga returned to his home, much to his parents' delight. Soon after, his father passed away. As was always the plan, Rana Sanga ascended the throne. Thereon, he worked tirelessly for 28 years as Mewar's ruler to ensure his people's freedom and fought many great battles to keep the Mughal empire

from expanding. Under his leadership, the Rajput clans united for the first time and his victories were why North India did not fall under complete rule of then Mughal emperor Babur.

The Battle of Haldighati

Akbar frowned. The Mughal emperor had just learnt of yet another failed attempt to win over the king of Mewar, Rana Pratap. It had been admittedly frustrating. Akbar would have rather had the Rajput willingly submit and express allegiance to the Mughal crown, but his commander Man Singh had returned bearing bad news.

While it upset the emperor, people in his court didn't seem too bothered.

"Did you hear," one joked, "he still calls himself the king of Chittor!"

"Of course, he is a king but without a kingdom," the other chuckled.

"Silence!" thundered Akbar. "You forget that Pratap has taken a fort that we had occupied until now."

Not only had Pratap indeed proclaimed himself the king of Chittor after taking the fort, but he had also ordered the people to not till their land until he said so and hanged a farmer for disobeying that order. This was an outright challenge to the Mughal rule as they had controlled the region after successfully capturing the Chittor fort (Chittorgarh) eight years ago in 1568.

However, Mewar was crucial to the Mughal empire's plans because it was only through this kingdom that it could access some of the most profitable trade routes to the ports in Gujarat and seas beyond to Arabia. It was also militarily important as any campaigns towards the Deccan or Delhi to Agra, to Gujarat, all needed to pass through Mewar. The kingdom was the most remote of all the Rajput kingdoms in Rajasthan, sharing borders with Gujarat and Madhya Pradesh. The Mughals had managed to capture Chittor, which was close to the Madhya Pradesh border, but Mewar still remained naturally separated from the rest of Rajasthan, thanks to the Aravalli Range mountains that stretched all the way from Delhi to Gujarat. This kingdom had a challenging terrain and it was in Akbar's interest to have it stable and allied with the empire. The quickest and most effective way would have been through manipulated friendship but it was now clear that a battle was unavoidable.

"Pratap considers all the other Rajput kings who have allied with the Mughal empire as traitors who have sold their honour," Man

Singh explained. "He has left us no choice but to crush him."

Akbar nodded, "Very well, then do it."

Standing tall at 7 feet 5 inches, the Rajput king scanned the horizon as his men brought in the latest report.

"Ranaji, our scouts say that the enemy has 80,000 men. They have cannons and guns."

"And we have only 22,000 soldiers and no guns," Rana Pratap calculated. The odds didn't look good but he was not going to admit that in front of anyone.

"I wish I had some cannons and more soldiers," he thought to himself.

Strategy was crucial if he was to fulfill his oath. He had sworn to win freedom for his people and reclaim Chittor from the Mughals.

His father, Udai Singh II, had once ruled Chittor, which had been Mewar's capital, but sensing the invaders' intention to capture it, he had shifted the capital to a newly-built city called Udaipur.

Rana Pratap remembered the day he had made this promise: "I swear that I will sacrifice my very life for Chittor. Till we attain freedom, I will not sleep on a bed but on the floor, and not wear rich clothes."

He had remained true to his word until now and absolutely intended to remain so until he fulfilled his goal. His men knew that and their respect for their king had only grown since then. They trusted him completely and were ready to put their best foot forward for him, no matter the cost.

Rana Pratap was an accomplished fighter and a shrewd strategist. Together with his followers, he had been a thorn in the Mughal empire's side for years. His guerilla warfare techniques had caused losses for the Mughals, the most recent being the fort the Rajput had captured on the outskirts of Chittor.

This time though the Mughals were confident that they would be able to finally subdue the Mewar king.

"This man must be stupid," Prince Salim scoffed when his spies reported Pratap's numbers to him.

Man Singh sharply retorted, "Not stupid, but brave! Don't be overconfident. He is a true Rajput. While huge armies and weapons do help in a battle, there is no substitute for courage when it comes to fighting."

Prince Salim rolled his eyes. "Enough of idle chatter. Let's attack and get this over with. I don't need to wait to swat him away like a fly."

"We can't."

"Why not?"

"Come with me and I'll show you."

With that, Man Singh walked out of the tent and pointed straight ahead of them. Past the dense foliage surrounding them lay a narrow path. Mountains towered on either side. The rocks and soil were a distinctly yellow colour

— like turmeric, known as haldi in the local language. It was what had prompted the name of the place: Haldighati.

"The way to Pratap's fort lies through that narrow valley aheadand you can bet that his men are waiting there to trap us. We would be easy targets. We will have to wait for them to attack first," Man Singh explained.

Yes, geography was on Rana Pratap's side and he knew it. It was a game of wait and watch. Minutes ticked by and hours turned to days. Yet neither side made a move. It was all beginning to weigh on the soldiers. The last thing any of the commanders wanted was for their men to lose motivation and alertness.

Prince Salim was now impatient. "We cannot wait indefinitely like this. Let's just attack."

Man Singh was about to dissuade him when one of the spies appeared to urgently report a matter. "Sir," he said, "I have found a long but easy path leading up to the fort."

This was welcome news.

"Take enough soldiers and attack the fort from the rear," ordered Man Singh.

The Mughal army wasted no time in marching ahead, ready to claim yet another victory.

Meanwhile, news reached Rana Pratap of the new troop movement. He was immediately

worried. "Ideally, we would have fought from the fort, but now it seems we have no choice but to fight in Haldighati," he mused. "Even if I ask for reinforcements from Udaipur, the city is nearly 50 kilometres away from the valley... we don't have time. We have to face our enemy right now if we want to have an upper hand."

Turning to his men, the king said, "Remember what you are fighting for. You are fighting for your freedom, our freedom. The right of our families, our children to live well, peacefully, not under the shadow of a foreign invader. We are not servants, nor shall we ever be!

Remember the sacrifice of Rajput daughters and sisters just so their fathers and brothers could keep their thrones. We shall never sell our souls like that. We are the Rajputs of Mewar, the bravest and most honourable of them all. Be proud, my men, for I am proud of you. Let us teach these Mughals a lesson they will never forget. We shall never bow before them!"

His warriors cheered, ready for combat. Rana Pratap turned to face Haldighati. It was now his best hope at cutting down Mughal numbers before more of them joined from the longer route. Taking a deep breath, he roared a single word: "Attack!"

Battle cries rang in the air as the two armies at opposite ends of the valley charged at each other. Swords and spears clanged making contact. Arrows rained from the Rajput side, finding their mark. The Mughals got their revenge by killing with their more sophisticated weapons. Still, it was no substitute for the Rajputs' skill. Rana Pratap himself was a formidable opponent. His armour weighed 72 kilograms and he always carried a spear and two swords, each weighing over 25 kilograms. More than 200 kilograms of weight on the man and yet he sliced through the chaos, wielding his weapons expertly as if they were lighter than a feather.

He was faster than the wind, thanks to his trusted horse Chetak.

The enemy lost heavy numbers just as the Mewar king had planned, but the favourable tide was short-lived as reinforcements arrived from behind the fort. The Mughal numbers overwhelmed the Rajputs. It did not escape Rana Pratap's attention. He had lost 15,000 of his people so far. Something needed to be done quickly to change the course of this battle.

"Man Singh!" it struck him. "He is an able commander but his death would demoralise his forces."

Spotting him on an elephant some distance away, Rana Pratap adjusted the reins to make his horse change direction. Chetak responded instinctively. He had always been in tune with his master and was known to be loyal only to him. People said that it was the horse who had chosen the king, not vice versa as was usually the case.
Word was that nobody could

control the majestic and powerful animal except Rana Pratap. Many said Chetak was as aggressive and skilled as his rider. He had been the king's fearless companion through many battles and was known to have a mind of his own. He immediately understood what the king wanted and galloped as fast as he could towards Man Singh.

By the time the elephant's driver recognised the frontal charge, the duo was too close. Although Chetak was smaller than the large elephant, but to provide his master with the necessary height, he planted his hooves on

the elephant's face. Rana Pratap then threw his spear straight at Man Singh.

"Arrrgghhh," groaned the elephant driver as the weapon pierced him instead.

The elephant swung the other way simultaneously, thus saving Man Singh in the process.

The commotion had attracted the attention of other enemy soldiers though and soon the Mewar king found himself surrounded. Close combat followed and despite his valiant efforts, Rana Pratap sustained several injuries.

Seeing their leader in danger, some Rajput soldiers rushed to his aid. Among them was the king's friend, Manna. He knew the king was in trouble. Surrendering was out of the question, as Rana Pratap was key in the Rajput resistance to the Mughal empire.

"Take the king and leave. Guard him with your life," Manna instructed some of the soldiers.

The Mewar king was weakened but was offended at the suggestion that he desert the battlefield.

"Of what use is your bravery if you are captured?" Manna reasoned. "You are not escaping as a coward. You are tactically retreating to save more lives and build a greater army. Survival is a must if our fight for freedom has to continue."

Others also echoed Manna's words. Rana Pratap gave in reluctantly. But before he left, Manna took the king's helmet and placed it on his own head. He was determined to provide a significant distraction so that the king could be escorted to safety. He was going to pretend to be the king. With that, he charged back into battle, ensuring that the enemy remained focused on him. Fooled, the Mughals managed to kill Manna – only to realise that the true leader was still at large.

In the meantime, Chetak had dodged enemy ranks and overcome challenging terrains and rivers to deliver Rana Pratap to the safety of the jungle. It was the horse's last valiant effort as he succumbed to a severe leg injury that he had suffered during the battle. Rana Pratap cried as his beloved Chetak breathed his last in his lap.

The following months were tough as the Mewar king was nursed back to health.

Saddened by the loss of his comrades and the lack of resources to rebuild, he considered submitting to the Mughal empire in a moment of weakness. However, the tribal leader of the Bhils, who had rescued the king and his family, offered hope and encouragement. More than that, he offered his own men. Financial aid came from a Chittor businessman named

Bhama Shah and, eventually, Rana Pratap was able to rebuild his army.

For the next 20 years, the Mewar king led the brave and powerful Bhil army to many victories. They reclaimed many forts from the Mughals and liberated the areas of Devar, Udaipur, and Komalmir.

Unfortunately, Rana Pratap did not live to see Chittor regain its freedom. But the people never forgot his message — never bow before invaders!

THE MAKING OF RANA CHATTRASAL

Thousands of flickering lights appeared over the hillside.

"That's a big battalion carrying torches!"

yelled a soldier, running to inform his superiors. "Chattrasal has attacked us."

As the Mughal army rushed forward towards the hill to defend themselves, they were surprised by two things. One was that the Bundela Rajput's attack actually came from the rear. The second was that the enemy forces on the hill were just cattle with torches tied to their horns!

While the news made Aurangzeb, the Mughal emperor, furious, it put a smile on a young, unassuming man's face. "They never seem to learn," he smiled to himself. "Good for us."

He would know. He had spent years learning about the enemy. His journey had started when he was only 12 years old.

"Who are you, son? What are you doing here in this jungle?" the old man asked the little boy. The light was fading quickly and it was worrying that a child seemed to be abandoned in the middle of nowhere.

To his surprise, the child responded, "First tell me who you are!"

The old man kindly replied, "I am Mahabali, the oil man. My village is close by. Is there any way that I can help you?"

"I am Chattrasal, the youngest son of Champatrai, the Bundela warrior," the child revealed. "My parents are dead."

The old man was surprised. He had previously worked for Champatrai and his wife Lal Kunwar. Something terrible had to have happened for such a brave warrior to lose his life, he was sure. He was right. Upon gently conversing with the child, he learnt how the Mughal army had surrounded his parents, leaving them with no choice but to surrender. It was against their honour to submit to the enemy and they chose death over that humiliation.

"I escaped," Chattrasal concluded. "Now, I need to get to my uncle's village. I will absolutely avenge my parents."

"I have no doubt that you will," Mahabali placed a reassuring hand on the child's shoulder. "But first, you should build up your energy for that. Come home with me, son. Eat and rest a while. Then proceed to your uncle's place. I will help you."

Trust was a rare commodity for Chattrasal at that moment. But he chose to trust in the old man nonetheless.

A day later, he left for his uncle's village.

The old man and his family marvelled at the child's quiet determination. He was very focused for someone of his age, that too after just losing everything — his family, his home, his entire lifestyle.

But Chattrasal was not in the habit of pitying himself. He was the kind of person who looked ahead and right now that meant getting to his uncle Sujanrai.

On the way, he came across two Mughal soldiers harassing devotees outside a temple. The anger inside him bubbled to the surface. "How dare these invaders treat us like this! Who do they think they are?" he seethed. He drew out his sword and charged at the unsuspecting soldiers. With one swing of his arm, he killed one of them. The other was momentarily stunned but his reflexes kicked in and he lunged at Chattrasal. The child was able to dodge the attack and deliver the final blow to the soldier.

That was the first day the public at large learnt his name, one that they all would come to remember and revere with pride.

"Who are you?" asked the devotees.

"Chattrasal," he replied, "son of Bundela warrior Champatrai."

"Long live Chattrasal! Glory to Chattrasal!" the people cheered.

The boy carried their blessings with him.

It was a long journey but eventually, Chattrasal reached his destination. Relief washed over Sujanrai as he saw his nephew alive and well.

"Thank God you're safe!" He drew him into a hug. "I was so worried that you had been captured too."

Chattrasal finally let his emotions flow as he was now with trusted family. He held on to his uncle for a few moments, longer than he'd done on earlier occasions. Sujanrai understood and patted him on the back. "You did well. Don't feel guilty. Your parents would have always wanted you to be safe."

Chattrasal nodded. He allowed himself to be led to a room to get refreshed and join his

uncle for a meal. As they walked together, Sujanrai casually asked, "What took you so long to reach here?"

"I had to pass through Mughal territory." With that, he also narrated the incident at the temple.

His uncle nodded. He wanted to have a deeper conversation with his nephew but decided to hold off for a few days and give him some time to come to terms with his emotions. Anger was a useful emotion but only if it was not the one controlling you.

A few days later, Sujanrai sat down with Chattrasal and formally asked him, "So, what do you want to do now?"

With a determined frown on his face, Chattrasal replied, "I must avenge my parents' death. I must build a Bundela kingdom."

"A worthy ambition," the uncle said. "But it is not easy to fight Mughal armies. You must first learn the art of warfare. There's far more to it than just knowing how to use your weapons."

And so began Chattrasal's training. He trained directly under Amar Singh, the commander of his uncle's forces. It was brutal and Amar

Singh certainly did not go easy on him, but Chattrasal was a dedicated student. Four years later, the young boy had shaped himself into a formidable warrior. Unfortunately, by then he felt that his uncle no longer shared his passion for going after the Mughals.

He was on the lookout for alternatives to fulfil his goal when by chance he learnt of his elder brother's whereabouts. Without informing his uncle, Chattrasal left to meet him.

Angadrai patiently heard him out. While he was on board with both taking revenge for their parents' death and establishing a Bundela kingdom, he felt that his younger brother had little patience. The timing was not right yet, he had surmised with all his years and skill in warfare. But Chattrasal appeared to be in no mood to wait. "We've wasted enough time already. I don't want to delay anymore," he kept saying.

"What shall I do to delay him a bit?" Angadrai wondered. Then he smiled as an idea struck him, "I know, I'll get him married! He'll have new responsibilities to consider and it will divert his mind for a bit."

So it was that Chattrasal married Devkunwar, the daughter of a Panwar feudal lord.

Time passed and Chattrasal was now back, again urging his brother into action. This time Angadrai was blunt in his response.
"I agree that we must get busy right now, but we should proceed only after due thought and consideration."

"What do you mean?"

"Before going to war, we have to collect enough funds and forces. Not only that, but we also need to study the Mughals' war strategy."

"How do we do that?"

"I've thought about this. Let's go to Raja Jaisingh. He's the chief of the Mughal forces but remember, nobody should be able to guess what our true intentions are."

Chattrasal did not like the idea of working with someone who had joined hands with the very enemy he wanted to bring down, but he knew

this was the best course right now.
So he agreed.

Jaisingh was no fool. He was suspicious of the duo's intentions given that they were the sons of Champatrai, but they managed to convince him to give them a chance.

Thereafter they were sent into several battles

and missions. It angered Chattrasal every time that they were fighting on behalf of Aurangzeb, the very man responsible for him losing his loved ones. Each time though, he took a deep breath and

reminded himself that this deceit was necessary. He mused, "Every day I learn how these Mughals think, work, plan and execute. Knowing their strengths and weaknesses is all I care about."

One day, they were assigned to Mughal commander Bahadur Khan. The mission was straightforward.

"Kurmamal, the ruler of Deogarh, has rebelled," he told them. "We have to lay siege to the fort he and his army are in."

"How long is the siege expected to be?" Chattrasal asked.

"According to our information, they have provisions for six months."

That was undoubtedly a long time to remain exposed to the elements while Kurmamal had a more solid and comfortable enclosure. The Mughal army definitely had the numbers to surround the fort and make sure new supplies to his army were cut off, but it was far too long. Chattrasal sensed an opportunity to completely win the confidence of the Mughals.

"I swear by my sword, the gates to the fort will be thrown open in two days," he declared.

Bahadur Khan was surprised but the Bundela brothers' reputation had preceded them, and he was willing to trust them with this chance. "I must make good my word," Chattrasal thought. "The fort is indeed strong – deep moats on three sides and just one gate that's closed and well-guarded. There has to be some entrance at the back."

He decided to keep an eye on the fort after sunset for possible clues. This night vigil paid off. He spotted a crack of light against one of the fort's walls - a secret entrance just as he had suspected!

The next morning, he asked the troops to remain alert as he tried to break into the fort. He rode into the moat on his horse and sneaked up to the wall where he'd spotted the opening. It was guarded but Chattrasal was able to easily subdue the soldier. The rest of the plan went as expected and the Mughal army conquered the fort!

Bahadur Khan was all praise and asked him to accompany him to Delhi where the emperor was keen to congratulate them. Chattrasal thought it would be another opportunity to learn something about the Mughals, so he went along.

The scene at Delhi unfolded quite differently though. Aurangzeb reserved his praise only for Bahadur Khan and

when he learnt the identity of the young man with him and what he achieved, all he said was, "Oh! The son of Champatrai should be happy that I have not ordered his beheading."

That comment did it. The Bundela Rajput snapped, "I don't beg for favours. I have my sword to help me take what is mine."

Enraged, the emperor ordered that Chattrasal be arrested but the Mughal soldiers proved no match for him. The young man escaped and headed south on his horse, determined to reach a leader he had heard of. Someone who had loudly declared the same objective as Chattrasal. Someone who was voicing what every person in the land actually wanted: Swarajya.

Days later, he was in the court of Shivaji.

"I got word when you left Delhi," the Maratha king said once they sat down for a meeting.

Chattrasal was amazed. "Really! Sir, your intelligence network must be unmatched."

Shivaji smiled at the compliment. He did not waste any time in asking his guest what the true purpose of his visit was.

"I want to help in liberating this land of the Mughals," Chattrasal stated, "and make it a place of Swarajya — self-rule. You know

everything about me and my circumstances I am sure, so you know I am driven to achieve this. My motivation and will have never wavered. So, what I would like to request is your guidance. How do I go about it?"

Shivaji looked him straight in the eye and replied, "Intelligently."

He explained that strategy and flexibility in actions and attacks would be key to defeating the enemy. "The Mughal army is strong in numbers. It relies heavily on that fact to win. But it always fails to withstand surprise attacks. We've benefitted greatly from this weakness of theirs."

Chattrasal nodded. Shivaji and his army's track record spoke for itself. No other king had defeated the Mughals as many times as the man before him. He had captured so many forts and regions from the enemy and crushed at least eight Mughal rulers. Yet this king sat humbly before him, determined to do more for his country. Chattrasal again voiced his desire to join Shivaji in this endeavour, but the Maratha king had different thoughts.

"Go home and free the people there," he said. "Create a kingdom free of these tyrants. I have full faith that you can achieve this."

"I have nothing, no resources," Chattrasal admitted.

"Build them. It's about finding the right people, the right opportunities, the right time. A brave and crafty warrior like you only needs to maintain a clear vision and plan."

As a parting gift, Shivaji Maharaj presented a sword to the young man. "I am sure you will never bring dishonour to this gift of mine."

Motivated by Shivaji's words, Chattrasal returned to his native land only to find that most of it was now under the enemy's control. Most local chieftains had become vassals of the Mughal empire. Surprisingly, even his own relatives were in no mood to challenge the foreign rule.

A leader cannot afford to be disheartened so quickly though. So Chattrasal worked tirelessly to speak with people, motivate them, and even rescue them many times. While he won the support of the general population and managed to scrape together a small army, he felt that it was not enough. For the first time, he began to doubt his decisions.

It made him restless and he wandered into the forest one night, trying to calm his mind

and pull himself together. He sighed inwardly, "I wish I had some sort of guidance."

Life answered his prayer quickly enough. To his surprise, he came across a small hut in the forest.

"I thought nobody lived here..." Curiously, he went to investigate it. He wasn't prepared for what came next.

"I have been waiting for you, Chattrasal," said the man sitting inside the hut.

For the first time, feelings of complete submission took over the warrior. He felt like he could trust this stranger. The man said he knew the doubts plaguing Chattrasal. He was confident that he would achieve his goal.

"But I need plenty of money to raise an army," Chattrasal pointed out.

The stranger simply replied, "That's my concern, not yours."

Though that answer was vague, it felt oddly reassuring to the Bundela Rajput. He finally asked the one question that was on his mind ever since he'd entered the hut, "May I know with whom I have the honour of speaking?"

"I am Pran Nath. You were desperate for a guru. I accept you as my disciple."

Chattrasal felt like a great weight had lifted off his shoulders. He now had the support that he had wanted. What his guru said next filled him with renewed hope and vigour. "Tonight, you have a task. Ride your horse and cover as wide an area as you can. That area will produce diamonds. You have my blessings."

So, the Bundela Rajput rode as he had never done before. Even his horse seemed to know what was at stake. It galloped tirelessly and fearlessly until the new day dawned. Chattrasal reported back to Guru Pran Nath in the morning, "I can't believe it! We did find diamonds, just like you said. There are more, I'm sure. We will need to mine them."

Chattrasal was ecstatic. Now his dream of defeating the Mughals was finally taking

shape. Soon, many men enlisted in his army and together, they freed many areas from the clutches of the enemy. The region of diamonds was named Panna and eventually Chattrasal made it Bundelkhand's capital.

Of course, Aurangzeb was not going to take it lightly. He ordered an army to march ahead and crush this uprising in Bundelkhand before it got out of hand. Oblivious to this threat, Chattrasal was out hunting with his trusted lieutenant Nathoo Singh. It was only the next morning that the lieutenant came back with disappointing news, "Maharaj, we are surrounded by Mughal soldiers."

The Bundela king had a trick up his sleeve. Nathoo Singh slipped away for a day as instructed and came back to report that all was ready as requested.

Anticipating an easy victory, the Mughals closed in on the king.

"Har Har Mahadev!"

The cries rang out all around them and the Mughal soldiers turned around, looking for the source. From the hills behind the enemy line, Bundelkhand's forces charged forward. Caught by surprise, the enemy suffered heavy losses and was forced to retreat.

"Aren't you ashamed?" thundered Aurangzeb when the news reached him. "The cheek of that brat — 5 horsemen and 25 swordsmen were all it took for them to defeat the great numbers of the Mughal army?"

Meanwhile, this event boosted Bundelkhand's confidence. The Mughals attempted many times to defeat Chattrasal, only for him and his people to emerge victorious every single time. He remained undefeated in the 52 major wars that he fought and maintained close

relations with the Maratha empire, which came to his aid in time of need. By the time he died at the age of 82, Rana Chattrasal had fulfilled his vows by killing the traitors who had cost his parents their lives and establishing a kingdom where people could live in peace and harmony.

www.ingramcontent.com/pod-product-compliance
Lightning Source LLC
Chambersburg PA
CBHW042136160426
43200CB00019B/2950